IMAGES
of England

CHESTER
DISTRICT

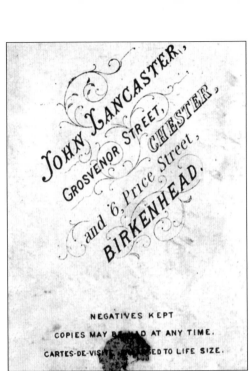

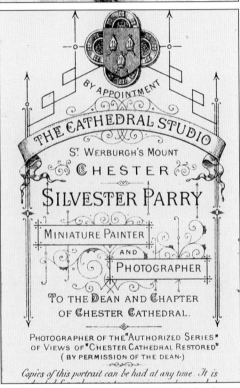

This size of portrait was known as a *Carte de Viste* and very popular in the 1900s. The back was ideal for the photographer to advertise on. Here are examples of them, taken by Chester photographers of that time; the female photographer must have been unusual! The young lady was Minnie Gwendoline Price of Picton, Cheshire.

IMAGES
of England

CHESTER
DISTRICT

Compiled by
Pat O'Brien

TEMPUS

First published 2001
Copyright © Pat O'Brien, 2001

Tempus Publishing Limited
The Mill, Brimscombe Port,
Stroud, Gloucestershire, GL5 2QG

ISBN 0 7524 2219 7

Typesetting and origination by
Tempus Publishing Limited
Printed in Great Britain by
Midway Colour Print, Wiltshire

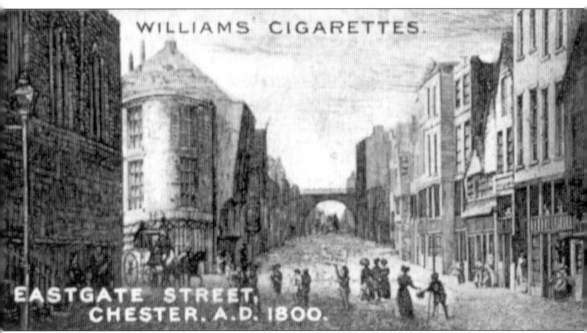

WILLIAMS' CIGARETTES.

EASTGATE STREET, CHESTER. A.D. 1800.

Since 1796 Chester held, possibly next to London, the reputation for being the largest manufacturer of tobacco in the country. The tobacco was consigned in very large quantities, not only to all parts of Wales, but also to the west of England, the Midlands, and the Northern Counties. This cigarette card is one of the second series of twelve views of Chester (as it was) issued by W. Williams & Co. in their cigarette packets.

Contents

The Right Worshipful the Lord Mayor of Chester and Admiral of the Dee, Reggie Jones.

Foreword

Dear Reader,

As Lord Mayor of Chester it gives me great pleasure to invite you to take a brief look into the history and heritage of our city, and to recognise the valuable contribution made by the people and places which have shaped and influenced the physical, sporting, and artistic culture of Chester for almost 2,000 years.

Nature has been kind in that Chester and its surrounding District is situated at the heart of the famous Cheshire countryside and nestles in the natural backdrop and beauty of the Welsh hills. Chester as a port has provided the stepping stone for early settlers with a sense of adventure to sail out to Ireland and the America's in search of their dreams. The River Dee has been the source of life for business and local fishermen while at the same time allowing us to celebrate our sporting culture by being the focal point for the recreational pursuits of sailing and canoeing and the more competitive regattas. The railway network in Chester has enabled good transport access to North Wales, the North West and the South of England and conjures up images of the great steam age now sadly passed into history.

The year 2000 heralded the Millennium Festival Trail which identifies forty of our most important buildings and provides the visitor with a unique opportunity to breathe in the development of Chester's architectural heritage. There is much to see and admire in the contrasting design and conservation of the urban and rural areas, which surround our city.

I hope that by reading this book you will find some of the treasured memories that make Chester so distinctive and special and that you will recognise and applaud the influence of those from the past in shaping Chester today. Enjoy Chester.

Reggie Jones, Lord Mayor
March 2001

TELEGRAMS: "BOLLANDS, CHESTER".   TELEPHONE Nos 755 & 756.   CHESTER,

Mrs Pollitt, The Knoll, Neston.   April. 19 34

BOUGHT OF R·BOLLAND & SONS, LIMITED,

CONFECTIONERS,
CATERERS,
WEDDING CAKE MAKERS.

BY SPECIAL APPOINTMENT TO
H.M. KING GEORGE V.

st. 1 Egg 3/6. 1 Novelty 1/3. Postage 6d. Sent to : Mrs Smith.   £   5   3

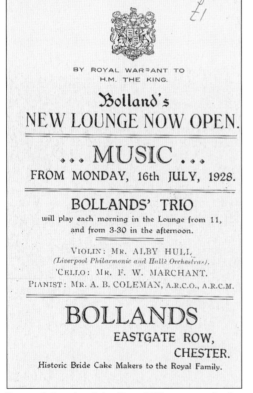

£1

BY ROYAL WARRANT TO
H.M. THE KING.

Bolland's
NEW LOUNGE NOW OPEN.

... MUSIC ...

FROM MONDAY, 16th JULY, 1928.

BOLLANDS' TRIO
will play each morning in the Lounge from 11,
and from 3-30 in the afternoon.

VIOLIN: MR. ALBY HULL,
(Liverpool Philarmonic and Hallé Orchestras).
'CELLO: MR. F. W. MARCHANT.
PIANIST: MR. A. B. COLEMAN, A.R.C.O., A.R.C.M.

BOLLANDS
EASTGATE ROW,
CHESTER.
Historic Bride Cake Makers to the Royal Family.

Painted details of the Royal Warrants, which can still be seen today on the front of the buildings they once occupied. *Top*: Bollands Billhead, *left*: Music Programme, *right*: Tea Lounge.

8

One
Leisure and Sport

in The Chester Watermen's Regatta was held at the end of each season for anyone who worked professionally on the river. It started from the waterworks and finished at the bandstand. The participants finished the day with a celebratory dinner at the Bar's Hotel.

Mill Weir. This is a rare view on a postcard of the east bank of the 'Groves' before it was landscaped and the bandstand built. It is postmarked for 5 July 1908 but the photograph could have been taken a few years earlier.

An advertisement card for Bithell Boats who were based at No. 2 Southers Lane opposite the landing stage that their boats operated from. The *Raglan* shown here in the early 1900s plied to Eccleston and Iron Bridge for Eaton Hall.

Bolland's Grove Cafe was a popular rendezvous for boaters and others. An advertisement in the *Observer* stated that customers' cycles could be stored without charge. Bollands were here from 1904 until closure in 1936.

Eccleston Ferry. This card was sent in October 1942. It shows the scene when boats used to drop passengers off for a snack in the nearby tearooms, a walk around the village, or a stroll back through the Meadows alongside the river to the city.

The Royal Agricultural Show. This view on a postcard shows the Royal Agricultural Show that was on the Roodee in June 1858. The foreground is the City Walls where Nuns Road is now, and shows the first grandstand that was built in 1817, and then replaced in 1899. This illustration was taken from a chromolithograph by John Mc Gahey (1845-1870).

Advertisement in the *Courant*, Wednesday 20 May 1903: 'Buffalo Bill's Wild West Circus, and Congress of Rough Riders of the World, headed by Col W.F. Cody (Buffalo Bill) will be on the Roodee on Friday the 29 May 1903. Included will be one hundred American Indians, who will re-enact many famous battles of the Wild West.'

This stand replaced the one built in 1815, (see p. 12). It was completely destroyed by a fire on 28 September 1985. The County Stand was originally built in 1900 at a cost of approximately £12,500.

Winner of the Chester Cup, 1907. The Chester Cup in 1907 was won by Querido owned by Frenchman, M.M. Chilaud. The jockey was J. Reiff, and the horse was trained in France. Querido was the 'Champion Horse of France', and won this race in a time of four minutes.

The Paddock; the parade ring is always a scene of great activity, giving the punter a close up view to study form in the flesh.

A scene in the late 1920s as horses and riders limber up before going back to the starting gate, opposite the Militia Barracks on the right-hand side.

First time round, passing the County Stand in the 1930s.

Crossing the Dee Bridge. This was a British Rail Standard Class unit 2-6-4T No. 80049 on a Chester-Rhyl train crossing the Dee Bridge at the Roodee. An accident occurred here on the 24 May 1847, when as the 6.15 p.m. train from Chester to Wrexham was crossing the bridge, the third arch collapsed, and the train fell into the river causing the deaths of five people.

This group of people were members of Chester Pageant assembled at the Diocesan Training Chester College in 1936. Bill Rowlands is third from the left front row, with Gerry Stockton standing next to him.

This is the Cycle Parade that was held in Grosvenor Park in 1910 to commemorate the Chester Pageant of that year.

Boughton Hall Cricket Club (Chester City). In 1873 Mr John Thompson a wealthy business man who lived at Boughton Hall decided to use part of his grounds as a cricket club, and thus the club was started. At first the games were against local sides such as Eaton Park Club and the 22 Cheshire Regiment. With experience they extended their fixture list to include the Liverpool and Warrington Clubs, and resounding defeats were inflicted upon them! Over the years the team has gone from strength to strength, and the facilities have been improved. The family ties can be seen when the team names are studied over the years, and this is the bond that makes it special.

Boughton Hall Cricket Club, the 1st XI, 1899. From left to right, standing: Wesson, -?-, Col Barter, H.J. Howell-Evans, E. Hodkinson, J. Henshall. Sitting: H. Hack, -?-, -?-, W. Jones, J.P. Douglas, W.A.V. Churton.

Boughton Hall Cricket Club 1st XI, 1906. From left to right: Wesson, J.P. Douglas, R.E. Birch, H.J. Howell-Evans, L. Hales, S. Blencowe, Wilson, E.H. Darby, Churton (captain), S. Donne, Revd Chignall, J. Henshall, H. Hack.

Boughton Hall Cricket Club, 1921. From left to right: G.A. Pratt, H.D. Roberts, J.H. Beilby, Mr Naylor, S.V. Hawkins, Capt. Symthe,-Osborne, L.N. Jones, Dickens, L. Hales, E.H. Darby, R. Frost, W.E. Jones, W.A.V. Churton.

William Edward Jones was born in 1888. In 1919 he joined Boughton Hall Cricket Club. By 1926 he became the first (and only) man to take ten wickets in an inning for Boughton Hall, when he had figures of 10 for 43 against Huyton. By 1927 he was captain of the Cheshire side. He retired in 1943.

William's brother, Leslie Jones, was born in 1891. He came to Boughton Hall Cricket Club at the same time as his brother. He later succeeded his brother as captain of the Cheshire side. His innings of 158 against Staffordshire in 1934 remained a record until 1950, when it was topped by Alan Vickery. He was obliged to retire on medical advice in 1939.

R.W. Barber was born in 1935 and at the early age of thirteen started to show his skills at cricket. He became a member of Boughton Hall in 1949 and was with them until 1967. He got his first captaincy for England, versus South Africa in 1960. Cricket was his life and his achievements could fill a book.

The late Mr Ron Fleet was a former president of Boughton Hall Cricket Club from 1992. His son Colin was also the team captain for many years.

Chester Nomads 1940/41. From left to right, standing: K. Starkie, R. Dain, R. Walley, W. Pritchard, R. Lloyd, A. Gooch, W. Harding. Front row: Hughes, C. Willets, A. Clegg, J. Powell, J. Raine.

Chester Nomads 1941/42. From left to right, back row: F. Hack, D. Keay, W. Pritchard, J. Darlington, A. Clegg, T. Light, R. Walley. Front row: R. Dain, O. Wright, K. Starkie, J. Powell, R. Lloyd, H. Harding.

The Victoria Rangers FC 1907/08. The photographer was W.A. Lamb, Victoria Road, Chester. The *Chronicle* reported on 12 September 1908 that they played Mission Athletic on the Roodee, and the result was Mission Athletic 4, Victoria Rangers 2. They played a good game and are to be commended on the sportsmanlike manner in which they took their defeat, which was by no means a disgrace to them.

The Chester College FC 1909/10. Up until the month of February 1910, they had won 15 games, lost 3 and drawn 2 – scoring 94 goals against 27 with 3 matches yet to play. This information had all been recorded on the back of this postcard sent by Will Barrett to his friend Reg Paul, at the School House, Ledbury, February 1910.

The Chester Rugby Club 'A' v. 'V' for the season 1928/29. Rugby started in Chester in 1870, but was not immediately very popular and did not continue. The Chester Rugby Club started in 1925, the first match was on the YMCA ground in Sealand Road against Chester College.

The Cheshire Lacrosse XII team represented Cheshire successfully against Lancashire and Yorkshire, and were unbeaten in 1928/29. They were winners of the Brooklands Trophy 1926/29, and the Juniors' Challenge Shield in 1929. Some of the team signatures on the back are: J. Crawford, C.G. Walkden, J.H. Bond, J. Whiteheart, C. Burgess and A.G. Bragg.

The Cheshire Hunt Point to Point in 1907 was held at Mr J. Hitchen's farm at Cholmondeston, near Church Minsull. Strict prohibition of betting gave the meeting the novelty of quietness.

Jimmy Walsh was born at Chester in October 1913. He won the light-weight championship of Great Britain on 24 April 1936 at Liverpool. He held his title until 23 June 1938, being beaten over 15 rounds on points by David Crowley at Liverpool. This is a cigarette card from a set of fifty boxing personalities by W.A. and A.C. Churchman.

Two
Into the City

The old Chester Castle Prison. The Prison Governor's house was the four storey half-octagonal building in the centre. The windows of the house overlooked the courtyards in which the prisoners were exercised. The prison was taken over by the Government in 1877, and closed seven years later.

Grosvenor Road. This postcard scene must have been taken from an old photograph before 1892 because St Brigid's church, seen on the left, was built here in 1829 after being transferred from Bridge Street and was then taken down in 1892. The tramlines are those of the omnibus that operated between Chester and Saltney.

Grosvenor Square. In this scene, St Brigid's church has gone, but the obelisk to the Revd Matthew Henry which stood in the graveyard (see above) is still to be seen in its original position. The centre poles that carried the overhead suspension for the electric trams can be plainly seen, whilst on the left stands the old Militia Barracks.

This was the old Militia Barracks built in the 1860s for the local militia. There was a secret tunnel that went under the road and came out in the dungeons of the old Chester Gaol; in case there was ever an outbreak in the prison it could be quickly dealt with from within.

The Parade Ground at Chester Castle, 1905. This was the period where most of the infantry Volunteer Battalions of the Army were trained in the use of bicycles as a means of transport.

The 1st Cheshire Engineer Volunteer Corps was raised in Birkenhead in 1860. In 1900 a contingent served with the Volunteer Force in South Africa. In 1907 they became the 2nd Cheshire Field Company Royal Engineers (T), and in 1914 were the first Territorial sapper unit to proceed to France.

Chester RE's Football Team. They were present in every major engagement, from the first Battle of Ypres to the Armistice, and a member of the 2nd Company. Corporal Jones, was awarded the DCM for bravery.

Regimental Police: reformed in 1920, as the 2nd (Cheshire) Field Squadron, RE (T), in the new Territorial Army they became the mounted sappers of the 2nd (TA) Cavalry Division, and enjoyed the distinction of being with the regular 1st Squadron, the only two horsed RE units in the British Army.

PLAYER'S CIGARETTES

CHESHIRE FIELD COMPANY ROYAL ENGINEERS, 1914

In 1939 the unit saw service in Palestine, Egypt, Syria, N. Africa and Italy, In 1943 they were renumbered 622 Squadron and equipped with Churchill AVs RE tanks they were turned into an assault squadron. The unit served in this role for the remainder of the war. This cigarette card was a fifty-card series of Uniforms of the Territorial Army by John Player & Sons.

Nun's Garden. In 1810 this archway was all that was left of St Mary's Benedictine Convent that had been built opposite Chester Castle in the Middle Ages. Some time after the Grosvenor Park came into being, the archway was re-erected there.

Grosvenor Park in Winter. The archway seen above is clad in a mantle of snow.

St Francis Procession, 26 May 1907 by the parishioners of St Francis, Roman Catholic church in Grosvenor Street. It was the first Catholic procession to be held through the streets of Chester since the Reformation.

Ticket, No.
120lb.
Cart, No.

1 July 1824.

Lamb-Row Machine.

From Rawlinson

For Mr Pate

	CWT.	QR.	LB.
Gross	52	3	
Sup. Tare	16	2	
Coal Munme	36	1	

A toll ticket. As there was no room for a weighbridge adjacent to the Wolf Gate, or in Pepper Street, it must have been sited outside Lamb-Row facing Pepper Street. The Toll Ticket is dated for the 1st July 1824 and issued by the Lamb-Row Machine.

This was the King's Head Hotel in its heyday, standing at the junction of Grosvenor Street and White Friars. This is an exceptionally fine advertisement postcard listing all its facilities. From the 1940s, the building started to deteriorate and was eventually knocked down in 1986.

Opposite St Michaels. Behind the tram on the street level is Robert Knowles, grocer, whilst above him on the Row is Thurman, Jackson & Co. Bootmakers. The tram is on its way to the General Railway s°tation.

From the 1870s until 1921 this was the Bishop's Palace. This is a postcard view of it in 1909. Before this the Bishop's Palace had occupied the site later developed as the King's School, (see p. 52). The Georgian building dates from the mid-eighteenth century, and is now Chester's YMCA headquaters.

The Convent School was opened in 1854 and in 1925 the Ursline Order of nuns, based at Crewe, took over the management of the school. This card was posted in Nantes railway station in France, 4 May 1934.

A distant view of the convent. On the left is the site of the Roman amphitheatre before excavation, with a pathway alongside the Convent wall leading towards St John's church. In the front of the garden, on the right, is where the City Cross was sited before being brought back to its original site outside St Peter's church.

This view of the school building and its church, was taken from the tennis courts, which were situated at the rear.

A close up view of the Amphitheatre Gardens, before any excavating was done. The tower in the background was part of the Lion Brewery in Pepper Street. All that is left now is the stone lion on top of the present day car park.

Against the background of Park Street, notice the level stretch of the city walls looking back towards the Eastgate. The Newgate was not built until 1938. The postcard was sent to Barmouth on the 29 March 1909.

Park Street. The sign on the wall where the cars are parked reads: 'Works, Anchor's Motors, Ltd Co., so the cars may be waiting to be serviced. The building on the far side of Pepper Street is Storrars the vet's, which was demolished in the 1960s for the NFU premises.

Newgate Street was known for over 600 years as Fleshmonger's Lane. The street used to run into Eastgate Street, by the Grosvenor Hotel. Except for St Andrew's United Reform church whose entrance is seen on the right, all these buildings were demolished in 1965, when it became Newgate Row.

Lower Bridge Street. The Dee Mill seen here beyond the Bridgegate had two four-wheeled horse-drawn delivery wagons. The drivers were old Tom Sinclair and Ted Weaver. Because of the steep hill, the drivers would crack their whips, and bellow at the horses to dash up it. When they got as far as Gamul Place, an oblong iron 'shoe' was slipped under the back wheels, and the horses rested before their final pull up to Castle Street.

Lower Bridge Street in 1810. On the right-hand side is the set of steps ascending to Gamul House. On the left is the east side of Lower Bridge Street between St Olave's church and Duke Street, once known as old Coach Row and nicknamed 'Rotten Row'.

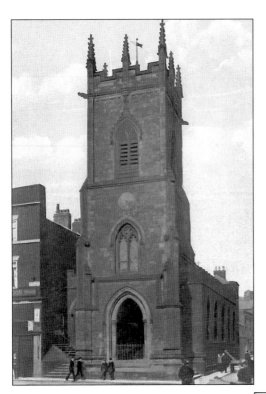

Beyond St Michael's church the buildings in Pepper Street are the former almhouses of William Jones which were demolished in 1948. In 1964 the Trustees of William Jones purchased the Nine Houses in Park Street and renovated them to carry on their traditions.

Mr Bailey, cabinetmaker found that the wooden effigy of King Charades was too tall to fit into the alcove, so a piece was taken out off the legs, and there was no further trouble! Mr Bailey's father can be seen on p. 68.

St Peter's church, between 1900 and 1904.

Hawarden Dining Rooms were situated at No. 47 Bridge Street. In Bennet's Business Directory of 1903, as well as an entry in the street section they also had an advertisement to attract the business community with facilities for functions etc. The proprietor in 1914 was Mr J.B. Marley.

A Great Western Railway Company delivery wagon outside the premises of Powell Edwards & Co. Ironmongers, and Thomas Cartright, Linen Draper and Hosier, situated on the west side of Bridge Street in the 1860s.

The Rows. This postcard view was produced in Germany before the First World War. The large brass plaque on the wall advertises Pegrams Teas, sold in the adjoining shop.

Providence Row. The south row of Watergate Street is not often seen on postcards. God's Providence House and the adjoining premises were occupied by G.H. Fennah's antique showrooms, whilst further along is the business of T.N. Richards.

God's Providence House. This is a folded-over postcard, the right hand side shows what God's Providence House looked like before it was restored in 1862. The pargeting on the front includes part of the coat of arms of Catherine of Aragon (pomengranates) because when she was married to Prince Arthur, she was the Countess of Chester.

This is one of the best-preserved medieval crypts in the city, and shows only a portion of the wine cellars. In depth they go down a further two floors and stretch down underneath the street as far as the premises of the City Press.

Leche House (1600) is the oldest house in Watergate Street. It still preserves its great hall, two floors in height, and on its east-side is a large fireplace with the family coat of arms over it. On the back wall is the grilled squint for keeping an eye on what is going on!

Bishop Lloyd's Palace. It is thought that both the ceiling and the fireplace may have come from the Bishop's Palace when it was situated in Abbey Square. This was largely destroyed by Parliamentry bombardment during the Civil War (1642-46). St Anselms (see p. 53) is said to have a similar ceiling.

43

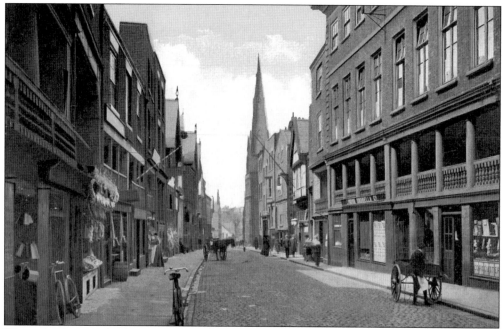

Watergate Street, which was once part of the main Roman Street (*Via Principalis*). In the early 1900s Watergate Street was no longer the busy thoroughfare it had once been. Shops identified on the right are those of a corkcutter, and the London Umbrella Company. Trinity church was founded in 1188 and its parish boundary plaque can be seen next to that of St Peter's church.

The buildings at the front of the Watergate have long gone. When Chester was a busy shipping port a toll on ships' cargo had to be paid at this gate, before being allowed into the city.

The Queen's School on City Wall Road moved here from Watergate Flags in 1883. The first Duke of Westminster in 1882 obtained Queen Victoria's permission for the school to add the title of Queen's. It received its grant of a coat of arms in 1936.

These are the pupils of the Queen's School who acted in a play entitled *Abu Hassan*, performed on the 3 December 1908.

From its inception in 1761 the Infirmary went through many changes in the nineteenth and early twentieth centuries. This is a mayoral group at the main door of the infirmary at the opening of the new extensions on 15 September 1912.

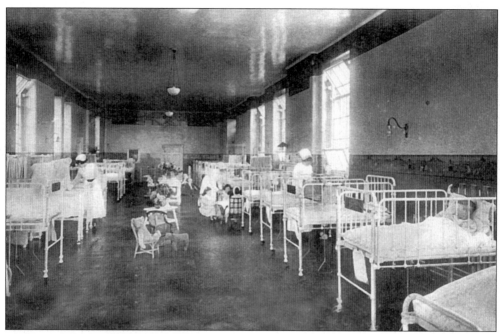

Children's Ward. The three uppermost windows of the children's ward that face City Walls Road, have a series of stained glass windows, with scenes depicting a day in the life of a young patient and entitled 'Morning, Noon and Night'.

Three

Environs of the Cross and Beyond the Northgate

The Old Cross. The corner of Eastgate Street and Bridge Street in the 1870s. The shop on the corner belonged to Mr Brewer, a brazier who sold, and probably repaired, buckets and tinware. The other shops are two butchers' shops with the meat carcasses displayed on hooks, following a haberdasher. The large building was occupied by Spencer, Woollen Dealer, Tailor, and Outfitter.

Eastgate Street, 1810. From medieval times the Row buildings at the north-west corner of Eastgate Street were known as the 'Butter Shops', where butter, milk, and other dairy produce were sold.

By 1905 street traders no longer obstruct traffic. This postcard was sent to Ontario, Canada at 9.05 a.m. on the 29 May 1905 and made its way back to Chester in 1999.

The Cross. The estimated date of this postcard is presumed to be between 1888-1903 – the corner buildings were not built until 1888, and electric trams were not introduced until 1903.

Having just passed each other on the loop in Eastgate Street these two horse trams are heading back onto the single tracks to continue their journeys.

Although the postcard says Southport, it is Eastgate Street. The view looks down from the Eastgate as a horse tram is about to go underneath on its way to the General Railway Station.

The No. 12 Tram on its way to Saltney is just passing Brownes of Chester.

The Eastgate clock shows the time to be 12.35 p.m. and looks down on a busy scene in the street. This postcard was sent to Southampton on the 27 June 1917.

The same scene thirty-two years later. A car is emerging from Newgate Street and a close up view of the grand and imposing entrance to Bollands can be seen.

The YMCA in 1907 was situated above Parr's Bank at the corner of St Werburg's Street and Eastgate Street. In 1921 Peter Jones, chairman of the YMCA, was instrumental in the acquisitioning of the old Bishop's Palace next to St John's church into which they moved.

St Oswald's church. Jutting out at the top of St Werburg's Mount, can be seen the south transept of the cathedral. From the early sixteenth century until 1881 this was St Oswald's parish church. The tower with the latticed window was the bell tower for the parish church.

Up to 1541 this was the Abbot's of St Werburg's private chapel. In October 1689, Bishop Stratford ordained Thomas Wilson in this chapel, a former King's schoolboy and a native of Burton, Wirral. Thomas later became a bishop; he was Bishop of Sodor and Man from 1697-1755.

The door into St Anslem's chapel is at the far end of the enclosed playground of the old King's School. From the window on the inside of the chapel is a wonderful view looking down onto the nave of the cathedral.

HMS *Chester* was originally ordered for the Greek Navy. She was built by Cammel Laird's of Birkenhead, launched on 8 December 1915, and the ship's fittings were completed early 1916. She was in the 3rd Light Cruiser Squadron, in the Battle Cruiser Force, and was the first casualty at the Battle of Jutland where many of the crew were killed or wounded and the ship was badly damaged. Her Battle Ensign is in Chester cathedral beneath a Roll of Honour Plaque.

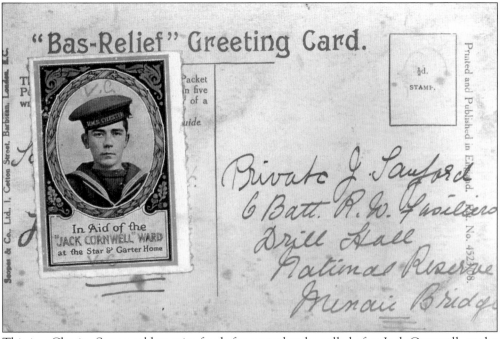

This is a Charity Stamp sold to raise funds for a ward to be called after Jack Cornwell, at the Star and Garter Home, in London. The VC was inserted by the sender afterwards, when news of his award became known.

A Cigarette Card. At the height of the Battle of Jutland, on 31 May 1916, the light cruiser *HMS Chester* was in action against four German cruisers. She suffered seventeen hits in a few minutes. One fifth of the ships' company were casualties. As she retired from the action, only one figure could be seen still standing by the forward 5.5 gun. It was the sight setter, young Jack Cornwell. The entire guns crew were either dead or dying, and Cornwell himself was mortally wounded but stayed at his post. He died of his wounds in Grimsby Hospital on the 2 June and was buried in a communal grave. Public opinion insisted that due to his bravery he be awarded the Victoria Cross. This was gazetted on the 15 September 1916, by which time his body had been reinterred in East Ham, London, after a funeral with full naval honours.

The Market Square, *c.* 1919. There are six Daimler buses and one Lacre bus, of the Crosville Motor Company at their departure points around the square. The destination board of the nearest one reads: Chester to Saighton, only.

King's School Cricket Club, 1902. From left to right, back row: W.A. Nayler, Revd T.J. Davies, H.J. Dutton (honourable secretary), S.M. Johnson, D.C. Jones. Middle row: -?-, C.M.D. Belton, C.E.Y. Sykes, W.M. Griffiths, G.H. Mason (captain), E.L. Marsden. Front row: R.H.C. Sykes, R. Robinson, M.R. Gardiner, E.V. Orett.

The Cathedral School was detached from the King's School from 1850-1977. This is the Cathedral Choir School around 1939. Canon Hardy who was headmaster and precentor of the cathedral is in the centre. Next to him wearing glasses is Doctor Middleton, organist and choirmaster.

Bill Rowlands was a probationer chorister of Chester Cathedral in 1939. When his voice broke in 1945, he was admitted to the King's School. After Army Service, he became a teacher, and taught at various local schools, ending up with a headship at Manley and Kingsley.

Old Northgate Street. In the *Strangers Handbook of Chester*, four inns and taverns are mentioned, amongst them the Legs of Man, seen here. The only one still surviving today is The Dublin Packet.

In this scene of Northgate Street around 1910, horse traffic is predominant. The policeman on point duty seems to be occupied with other matters.

This was the Via Decumana (the street of ten men) called after Roman gate, Porta Decumana. Prominent in this postcard is the ancient coat of arms of the city with its motto, *Let the Ancients Worship the Ancient of Days*. The card is postmarked 10.30 p. m. 31 July 1909.

Clemences was once a long narrow shop which led to an array of fine cheeses, some stacked high on shelves, some packed ready for delivery and some cut ready for sale. With sawdust and straw on the floor, there was a flavour of the farm about the place!

In the 1896 Trade Directory the buildings listed were: the new Town Hall (see above in 1900), and on the opposite corner of Princess Street were the Coach and Horses Hotel, the Elephant and Castle public house, and William Hewitt, coach and carriage builder. By 1902 the latter had changed to J.A. Lawton & Co. but the business was the same.

On Wednesday 1 July 1903, the Lawton Carriage Factory was completely destroyed in a fire. This is a view taken from the front, in Market Square; part of the flaming debris fell into the stables at the rear of the Elephant and Castle and ignited bales of straw there.

Field Marshall Lord Robert came to Chester in August 1904 to unveil a memorial in Chester cathedral in memory of officers and men of the Cheshire Regiment who were killed in the South African War 1898-1902. He arrived on Friday 5 at 7.00 p.m. by train from Lancaster and was met at the General Railway station by the Duke of Westminster in his capacity as Lord Lieutenant of the County.

After a night's stay at Eaton Hall, Lord Robert and his entourage were driven to the town hall on Saturday morning for a civic reception and afterwards proceeded to the cathedral for a service to unveil the war memorial.

This was the scene from the Sunday School Pageant held every year. The parade would assemble outside the Town Hall behind their parish church banner and march through the streets to the Roodee for a special service. The banners of the parish of Saltney and All Saints, Hoole, can be plainly seen in this view.

Empire Sunday Military Parade took place on the Sunday before the second Monday in March each year, because Monday was the official Empire Day. The name derives from the assistance given by the Colonies in the Boer War. In 1959 the name Empire Day was changed to Commonwealth Day.

The Prince and the Princess on the 6 July 1908 on their way to the Town Hall for a Civic Reception. Part of the mounted escort were members of the Cheshire Yeomanry.

Mr Edward Paul was chairman of the family's flour milling company, Paul's Mills of Liverpool and Birkenhead. His opponent in the two General Elections of 1910 was Mr R.A. Yerburg, the sitting candidate, Conservative Party. In the election on 17 January Mr Yerburg won by 202 votes; he also won the second election in December.

This group of ladies belonged to No. 1 Army Remount Depot, the first to be run by women. Their depot and the stables for the horses were in Crane Street. They trained the horses on the Roodee, and in nearby streets. This photograph was taken after a reception in the Town Hall in 1919, prior to being disbanded.

The Chester Cocoa House Ltd started in the Market Hall in 1882, at this time they also had branches in Bridge Street and Foregate Street. By 1892 they had seven establishments, but by 1930 this was reduced to four or five. In 1939 there were two – the Market Hall and Brook Street. All that remains now are the premises at the corner of Brook Street by Hoole Road Bridge. This still has 'The Chester Cocoa House Ltd' embossed in stone on the front.

Listed in Phillipson and Golder's Directory for 1920-1921, is E. Robinson, undertakers, in Abbey Gate off Northgate Street. Also listed is Duttons, undertakers of Frodsham Street, agents for metallic air-tight coffins.

This section of the Wall is to the east of the Northgate. Where the rough stones commence, and spreading to the left is the Roman Wall. The plinth which indicates the top, appears as four straight edges, partly covered by the top of the ivy. The wall is thirteen courses of stone, 22ft high, or 6.70 hectares. At the bottom there is a ditch 20ft wide, and 9ft deep in a V shape.

The Flying Fox was acquired in 1913 and was used on the bus route between Chester and Ellesmere Port. This service was started by Crosville Motors Co. in 1911. Its fleet was originally No. 5, later becoming No. 19. It had a Daimler CC chassis and had 23 seats; the registration number was DU 2207 and was sold in 1927.

Late in 1906 Crane House and warehouse was rented to G. Crossland Taylor, the founder of Crosville, from the Shropshire Union Railway and Canal Co. who built a modern machine shop to assemble motor cars. This was to become the nucleus of the repair and assembly shops of Crosville Motor Services. They also sold tyres made at their Helsby Works and even re-built engines for the *Bend Or* and *Ormonde* steam boats.

This scene was in the Dee Basin in 1913. The gentleman in the boat with the bowler hat is Joseph Harry Taylor, boatbuilder. His son Wilfred Taylor is on the oars and Joseph Horace Taylor is in the bow. In the background is the stable block for the canal horses, and the watertower.

There were once two small shipyards adjacent in the Canal Basin. William Roberts Yacht Yard, specialised in large pleasure craft, such as the *Ormonde*, and the *Bend Or*, for the Dee Steam and Motor Boat Co. Ltd. In 1906 they built the hull for a large motor boat for Crosville Motor Services Ltd. The Taylors' boatyard produced canal craft and fishing boats, especially salmon boats for the River Dee.

Thomas Bailey, a boilermaker by trade, was the gaffer of a shipyard to the left of where the canal enters the River Dee. He lived in the top two floors of a three-storey house next to the tent makers (Davies) on the quayside. He died around 1890 when he was about sixty years old, falling down the stairs in his house and breaking his neck.

Building a boat in the Dee Basin, *c.* 1914. William Howard has his hand on the funnel. Standing on top of the cabin of the narrow boat *Swan* is the gaffer with his coat on and hands in his pockets.

This is the drydock in 1920. Joseph Horace Taylor is working on *Betal* which belonged to Harris Barges, whose director was Mr Pinfold.

This is one of the fleet of narrow boats owned by the Shropshire Union Railway and Canal Co. heading out of Chester towards Ellesmere Port. In 1921 the SURC Co. still had a fleet of over 200 canal narrow boats.

This photograph was taken outside the Northgate locomotive sheds in the mid-1930s. On the far left in the back row is Manley, and in the front row, third and fourth from the left, are Phillips and Harry Randall.

Because of its proximity to the Roodee, Northgate station had a large number of racegoers. On race days express trains of fifteen coaches each were laid on between Manchester Central and Northgate station. Because of the length of these trains, the arrival departure platforms had to be extended in 1905 and 1911.

Liverpool Road station was on the Chester Northgate to Connah's Quay line. It was opened on 31 March 1890, and the other stations were Blacon, Saughall, Chester Golf Club, Shotton and Connah's Quay. It closed on 3 December 1951.

The mill was built in 1777 and in 1869 the miller was William Carter. At some point in the 1890s a family called Dean became the millers and it remained with them until its closure in the 1950s. They also operated a bakehouse attached to the mill. After the mill ceased working the bakery moved to Saltney. In 1984 the mill was converted into a five-floor residence.

Thomas Hunt built Mollington Hall for his family in 1756, after bringing together the two principal estates of Mollington township. From 1797 the house was owned and lived in by the Feilden family, and they sold it in 1907 to T. Gibbons Frost Esq. (see p. 81). In 1929 it was again sold and the estate finally broken up, but the new owners never took up residence. After being empty for several years, the hall was demolished in 1938.

Church Road, Saughall. The set of steps on the right is the public footpath to Shotwick church. These footpaths started out as 'Corpses Way', the shortest way to the parish graveyard, and once used became a public right of way.

Saughall station was opened on the 31 March 1890. The station was on a section of the Grand Central Railway from Chester to Hawarden Bridge, and closed on 1 February 1954.

Swinging Gate Pub (on the right), looking down Hermitage Road in 1907. The pub's sign has this verse:

This gate hangs well,
It hinders none,
Refresh and pay,
And travel on.

Backford church contains several items of interest. It has a chained Bible, the second oldest in Wirral, which was printed in 1617. The sanctuary chair north of the altar, used by visiting bishops, is made from altar rails which were in the church 300 years ago. There are rare hatchments done by Randy Holmes III; because his work was not licensed by the College of Heralds, it was destroyed in all the other churches, except here and Stoak church.

The place name Stoak or Stoke goes back to Anglo-Saxon times, meaning a stockade or fortified camp. At one time the rights of burial for Stoak people belonged to a church at Chester because it was part of its parish.

Elton village. This postcard has the postmark of Ince, 6 December 1910. The large farmhouse on the rock is still there. Before the railway line was built, the land at the back was part of Ince Marshes which run down to the Mersey Estuary – the rock would have given it a dry foundation, and would have protected it if the marsh got flooded.

Ince and Elton station. This branch line between Helsby and Hooton was opened on the 1 July 1863 by the Birkenhead, Lancashire and Cheshire Junction Railway. The station was then called Ince, but on the 17 April 1884 it was renamed Ince and Elton. The view is looking towards Helsby.

The village of Thornton-le-Moors has not changed much since this postcard was sent eighty-nine years ago on the 6 April 1911, from Helsby. Does anyone know who the gentleman with the cycle was?

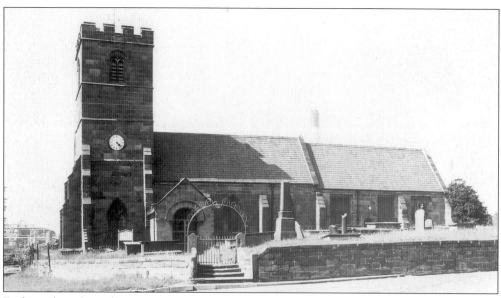

Dedicated to St Helen many years ago, the parish church of St Mary Thornton-le-Moors occupies the site of a Saxon chapel known to have existed prior to the Norman conquest. In the rectory close by, Bishop Lloyd who had a house named after him by his daughter in Watergate Street in Chester (dated 1615), died in 1614.

Four

Districts outside
the Eastgate

The City of Chester's police were not incorporated into the county force until 1949. The city police used the town hall as their offices, until the new headquarter's building for the county force was opened in 1967. Opposite the south-east corner of City Road is the former Cheshire Police headquarters of 1884, designed by John Douglas.

These are some of the postmen, telegram boys and civilian staff outside the main post office in St John Street posing for a postcard photograph, dated 21 March 1907. All that is left of this grand entrance is the small stepped cornice after the letter E, next to the drainpipe.

The building in the background is the old post office sorting office opposite the General Railway station (the building is still there) which opened in 1912. Before vans were acquired by the post office for delivery purposes, the weight of parcels could not exceed 10lb. With the use of motor vehicles, the weight was increased to 15lb. In 1935 this new fleet of vans went around the city in convoy, with a parcel on the roof to inform people of the new weight allowance.

Only an artist's sketch can present a full view of what the Blossoms Hotel used to look in its heyday. There has been an inn on this site since 1410, which was destroyed in 1643. William Bunbury of Stanney then built another inn named Blossoms, which opened in 1650.

The name 'Blossoms' is derived from St Lawrence the Deacon who was an early martyr. After his death his admirers surrounded the corpse with blossoms. The terminus for the Chester stagecoach in London was the Blossoms in St Lawrence's Jewery, so the stagecoach went from one Blossoms Inn to another.

King Charles Tower. Before the coming of the railways the Chester Canal was the principal trade route in and out of the city. Heading out into the Midlands is this horse drawn barge. Sometimes on the rope leading to the horse there would be a smaller length hanging down dragging an old boot to fool the horse into thinking the boatman was walking behind him.

From the old Cow Lane Bridge the former Mill Quay can be seen on the right stretching as far as Union Bridge. All the tall mill buildings on this side have gone, except for Frost's Steam Mill in the distance. On the left is Griffith's Mill (see p. 81).

This was Griffith's Mill (now the Mill Hotel), c. 1890. The gentleman in the doorway is Mr Millington, a relative by marriage of the Taylor family who were boatbuilders. The boat is facing Union Bridge.

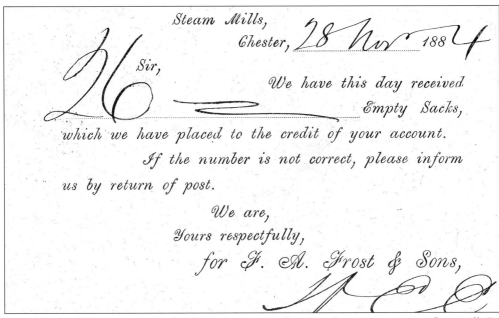

Steam Mills,
Chester, 28 Nov 188 4

Sir,

We have this day received

Empty Sacks,

which we have placed to the credit of your account.

If the number is not correct, please inform

us by return of post.

We are,
Yours respectfully,
for F. A. Frost & Sons,

In 1819 a local family converted a disused cotton mill in Boughton into a steam flour mill. By 1854 the firm became known as F.A. Frost & Sons. This is one of their printed account cards for the return of empty sacks, dated 28 November 1884. Other flour mills were Albion and the Cestrian (established in 1868-1869 by John Wiseman), and the Queens in the early 1890s by Messrs Griffiths.

This is an artist's impression of what Foregate Street may have looked like in the early part of the nineteenth century. This is a part of 'Roman Watling Street' heading in a curve northwards. This postcard was issued before the First World War.

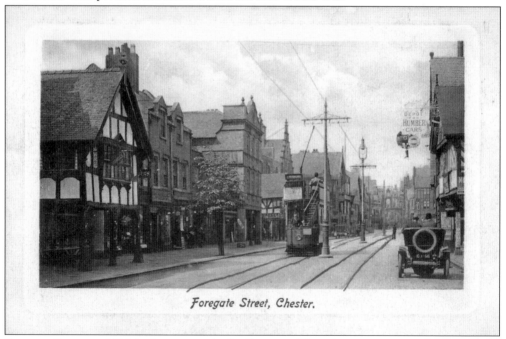

Foregate Street, Chester.

Foregate Street in 1908 looking towards the Eastgate. The advertisement on the tram is for Duttons, Sigarro Stores, Eastgate Street. The message on the back says; 'Came here on the way to Keswick on our motor tour at the age of 11 years 1 month with Mother, Father, and Phil.'

The NAFFI Club was situated in Love Street in what was once part of Forest House, the nineteenth-century residence of Col. R. Barnston who became the Colonel of the Chester Local Militia in 1803. After its NAFFI's days it became the Co-op's tearooms and today it is a night club.

Looking towards the Bars, on the left, is Ellis's Cestrian Piano Stores, on the corner of Queen Street with the Globe Boot Company next door. Publisher, Phillipson & Golder, Stationer, Chester.

Postmarked 21 July 1917. The shops include: No. 50 Foregate Street (on the left), is James Hunter Ltd, agricultural seed merchants; No. 48 is Little Nag's Head, Cocoa House, (see p. 64) the manager was C. Stewart; No. 46 Guest & Wardle, cabinet makers and upholsters; No. 44 P. Lawson, Royal Hotel and garage; opposite this at No. 37 is G. and W. Morton, boot and shoe manufacturers.

This bus joined the fleet of Chester Corporation buses as No. 44 in September 1942. It was a utility Guy Arab chassis with a Massey bodywork working on the Eaton Hall service, which served the Cadet School based there (see p. 120). The route went via Foregate Street, Handbridge, Eccleston Village and Eaton Hall. It was withdrawn from service August 1954.

This is the 'Fountain' junction at Boughton in January 1907, soon after the opening of the electric tram routes. On the left is No. 10 outbound towards the Tarvin Road and on the right is No. 2 inbound from Christleton Road.

Walmoor College, Chester Cookery Class.

In 1921 Walmoor Hill the former residence of John Douglas, an architect whose work is still admired throughout the city, became Walmoor College, a school for young ladies. The principal between 1930-1931 was Miss E.C. Butterworth. The school remained as Walmoor College until 1933.

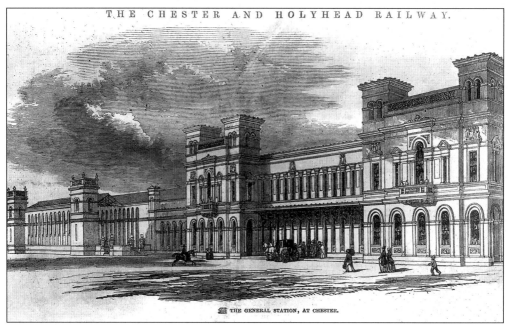

THE GENERAL STATION, AT CHESTER.

The Chester and Holyhead Railway started in 1840. They were one of four railway companies to have the station built. After a board meeting on the 18 March 1859 they decided, due to financial difficulties, to amalgamate with the London North Western Railway Company.

This photograph was taken in March 1903 alongside the Queen Hotel when the first electric tram was given a trial trip; this is tram No. 5. A fleet of twelve new trams replaced the horse trams; they were quite small vehicles being only 24ft long, with a 14ft saloon. There were 20 seats, while 23 places were provided outside on reversible 'garden' seats, with no overhead cover.

The Strike Committee, 1911. A series of disjointed strikes in the Summer of 1911 prompted the four leading unions to seek intervention by the Board of Trade and when this failed an official strike was called on 17 August. The following day Northgate station closed down. A squadron of the 16th Lancers and soldiers of the Wiltshire Regiment were brought to Chester and encamped on the Roodee. The strike ended on 19 August when a Royal Commission was set up to resolve the dispute.

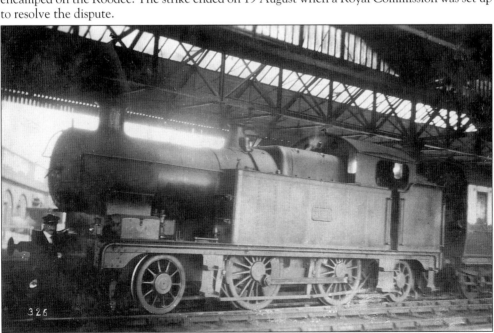

This is the Great Western Railway engine No. 3629 2-4-2T with the Down Birkenhead (Woodside) at Chester General station.

This is the Royal Train passing through Chester General station on 15 July 1937. It is hauled by Royal Scot class 6P 460 Loco. No. 6152 'Royal King's Own Dragoon Guardsmen'. The royal train was comprised of an ex-LNW railway stock with painted white upper panels and carmine lake lower panels. The Queen was in the third coach and was waving to the crowds from the window. When this photograph was taken it was raining heavily and the light was very dull.

This is Chester General railway station on the 29 August 1964. These are two of the station pilot engines used for shunting and standby duties. They are LMS 4F-0-60 No. 44389 and LMS 3F-0-60T No. 47669.

The first tree to be planted in Chester district to commemorate the Coronation of King George V was at Newton-by-Chester. At 9.00 a. m. on Coronation Day in bright sunshine, a cedar tree was planted by Mrs C.A. Griffin, wife of Revd C.A. Griffin. The tree was planted on the Flookersbrook estate facing Hoole Road. The grounds of their house 'Folly' were used for sports events also commemorating the Coronation.

A class from Hoole and Newton Elementary School, *c.* 1932.

Hoole Road started out in the late nineteenth century as villa residences for some of the city's more prosperous citizens.

Looking out onto Hoole Road – the building on the left-hand corner is No. 56, now Ba-Ba guest house, whilst the large building on the right with the roof jutting out was Hoole fire engine house, 1915-1916. This district originally lay outside the city boundary; in 1894 it became Hoole Urban District, and was eventually absorbed into Chester City in the mid 1950s.

Leonard Cheshire was born on the 7 September 1917 at No. 56 Hoole Road, Chester. He was the son of an Oxford Don and has been cited as being the greatest bomber pilot in any air force. By a strange coincidence, his best friend at Stowe in the 1930s, Jack Anderson, and also his close friend at Merton College, Jack Randle, were also awarded VCs. In 1936 he joined Oxford University Air Squadron, and decided to fly bombers rather than fighters. He took part in over a hundred operational flights during the war, winning the DSO (and two bars), the DFC and ultimately the Victoria Cross. He also received the Order of Merit, the highest civilian decoration the sovereign has to bestow. By the time he died, he left a unique living memorial – 140 Cheshire Homes caring for 10,000 disabled people. (Photograph: ref No. PC 76/23/31 is from the Royal Air Force Museum Collection and has been reproduced with permission.)

The Bird-in-Hand Inn is believed to date back to 1500 although no early records have survived. Towards the end of the nineteenth century the inn was described as an old Elizabethan type of building with a thatched-roof, but shortly afterwards it was destroyed by a fire and had to be completely rebuilt. From 1815 until 1974 there were fourteen licensees registered in the County Trade Directories.

Mickle Trafford station in 1911. This is an excursion train bound for New Brighton via Chester. The station opened in 1899, but closed for passenger trains on 12 February 1951. (A. Willis collection)

The White Horse Inn, seen here on the Main Street, first opened in 1822, and is still in business today. The publican in 1869 was Elizabeth Leech. The postcard is dated 11 June 1911, the Coronation year of King George V. The parish magazine records that they had a lot going on that year!

BARROWMORE HOSPITAL,
GREAT BARROW,
CHESTER

In the early 1920s, Barrowmore Hall became the East Lancashire Tuberculosis Colony, and later with extensions became Barrowmore Village Settlement providing work homes and training for disabled people. On the 29 November 1940, the former sanatorium was destroyed by a landmine resulting in the deaths of thirty-two patients and staff. In 1947 it became Barrowmore Hospital and has now closed down.

Canon Lionel Garnett, the rector from 1869-1911, started the Flower Service at St James parish church, Christleton. It is held on the nearest Sunday to the Feast Day of St James, its patron saint. This is the Flower Service, 1908.

The Canal Bridge. In Victorian times, when canal boats were heading in for Chester on Saturdays, they were not allowed to proceed onwards after 6.00 p. m. – they had to remain in Christleton until after 6.00 p.m. Sunday.

Tarvin Mill – there are records of a mill being here since the thirteenth century. It operated on a stream coming from Willington, and was working until sometime in the 1920s. The miller in 1869 was Thomas Williams.

OLD COTTAGES, TARVIN.

This lovely group of period houses is in Church Street. The photograph was taken over seventy years ago and the Church Cottages can be seen next to the parish church of St Andrew. Together they enhance this ancient and beautiful town.

Station Hotel, Mouldsworth. No. 3.

The Station Hotel, Mouldsworth has the licencee W. Houghton, as the landlord in the 1923 Trade Directory. Until 1955 the Catholic population of the area worshipped in a pavilion at the rear of the hotel. A church was built on nearby Station Hill that year. In the early 1980s the Station Hotel changed its name to the Goshawk.

The Old Toll Bar, Nr. Kelsall, Delamere Forest.

The adjustable pole that used to stretch across the road at Toll Houses had the metal end of pike shafts stuck in it to prevent gentlemen on horseback jumping over it, and thus avoiding paying the toll. Hence the name 'turnpike'.

The village of Duddon has a famous ghost at the 'Headless Woman' pub. At one time a headless figurehead off a ship stood in the pub's garden, but it has long since gone. This was formerly the figurehead of the sailing ship *Falkirk* which sailed around the world for many years.

In 1869 Thomas Jones was the blacksmith of Kelsall. This view is from a postcard dated 11 September 1923, and is from a set called the 'Beeston Series' published by F.H. Haines, Art Studio, Tarporley.

Huxley lies six miles south-east of Chester in the rural area between the roads to Whitchurch and Nantwich. It has two old manor houses in the village. The oldest, Higher Huxley Hall has a carved Elizabethan staircase, two priests' holes, and a south facing 'Leper' window. It is said that a ghostly lady rides a white horse at midnight through the horsewash.

Huxley Mill was on the River Gowy; it had an undershot waterwheel. The mill was attached to Huxley Mill Farm on the estate of Lord Henry Cholmondely in 1868, the miller at that time was John Bate. John was also the miller in 1861, but by 1886 it had passed to Thomas Bate. Milling appears to have stopped by 1914.

This view of Burwardsley was taken 1910-1911. It was printed in Germany and published by Aston of Tattenhall. Most of the farms and houses belong to the nearby Bolesworth Estate Company who administer it on behalf of the Barbour family who were originally in the Cotton Industry in Manchester.

School Valley, as seen from over the school playground wall, early 1900s.

From 1901-1905 Plovers Mass in Delamere was the training area for the Earl of Chester's Imperial Yeomanry. The regiment provided two companies in the Boer War, the first company was commanded by Lord Arthur Grosvenor, son of the first Duke of Westminster.

Burwardsley Road, Tattenhall.

Here is a mounted troop of the Earl of Chester's Imperial Yeomanry on an exercise passing through the village of Tattenhall before the First World War. The postcard was printed in Berlin.

This view is from the High Street looking towards Burwardsley Road. On the right-hand side are the Nine Houses and the Sportsmans Arms; the licensee in 1907 was Mrs Mary Challinor. This postcard was posted in Tarporley in 1904.

Postmarked Tattenhall 29 May 1906, this view shows the north-east part of the village looking up the High Street from the war memorial towards the village centre. The ancient Manse is the white building on the left, demolished over fifty years ago.

This view was from Church Bank, looking down the High Street in the 1920s. This postcard was published by A.W. Aston's newsagents and tobacconist, whose shop can be seen here. It was No. 1 in Aston's New Series.

A distant view of Beeston Castle from Tattenhall Lanes. This is one of Aston's New Series and is numbered No. 13 and is postmarked 8 April 1915.

Handley, this view looks south from the church. The black and white cottage on the right is said to date from 1601. In the background is the Calveley Arms which was once a coaching inn. The landlords were Maria Done, 1822-1827 and James Dean in 1828.

Handley, looking north towards the church. This postcard is part of the same series as above, the 'Perfection' series issued around 1910-11.

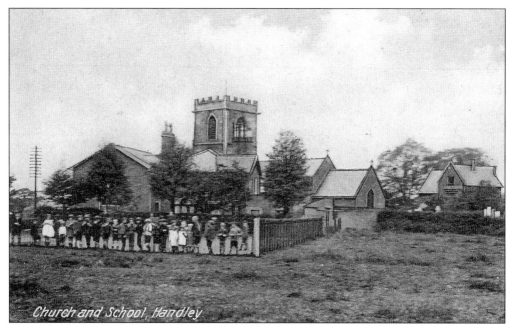

Church and School, Handley

With the parish church of All Saints in the background, pupils of the church school pose for the photographer. The perpendicular west tower is dated 1512; the west face is the oldest surviving part. When rebuilding the church in 1854, James Harrison spared the beautiful nave roof of 1661 with its hammer beams, arch-braces and collar beams.

CUDDINGTON. CHESHIRE.

Cuddington was linked with the nearby village of Sandiway in 1935. A local foxhound named Blue Cap was entered for a speed trial at Newmarket in 1743 and won. One of the local inns was named after him.

Edge Mill near Malpas in 1907. There were three medieval water mills in this area at the same time, operating off the same stream. This mill was known as Edgehall and had its wheel removed around 1810. The miller in 1869 was George Price and in 1895 was George Hughes.

OLDHALL STREET, MALPAS, CHESHIRE.

St Malpas, Oldhall. The Red Lion Inn is the last building on the right-hand side. In 1834 this was the posting and excise office and was at that time in the charge of James Peach.

This is the High Street, Malpas in 1908. Some of the pub's landlords ever the years have been: The Crown Hotel – Jane Reeves (1822-1823), Thomas Lewis (1824), Thomas Shaw (1825-1828); The Red Lion – Ann Shaw (1822-1823), James Peach (1825-1828).

The Cross, Malpas. The Wynstay Hunt took its name from the residence of the Wynn family who started it. An extract taken from the Hunt Diary, 11 January 1872 reads: 'Met at Malpas, found a good fox at Edge, and killed him close to Aldersey Hall in the open, found again in Castletown, and had a first class gallop to the Cheshire Hills. Home late, but the best day of the season.'

Ox Hayes, Malpas. The derivation for Ox Hayes (Ox Hey) is 'enclosure for oxen'. In the 1851 Tithe assessment for Old Castle, there is a field named Ox Pasture.

Malpas station opened on the 1 October 1872 and closed on the 16 September 1957. It was situated on the London North Western Railway branch line from Tattenhall Junction to Whitchurch.

Dymock's Mill, near Malpas. This mill had two waterwheels, one said to be in Cheshire, and the other in Flintshire. Both of the wheels were undershots and parallel to each other; each wheel drove a pair of stones. The mill ceased work around 1930.

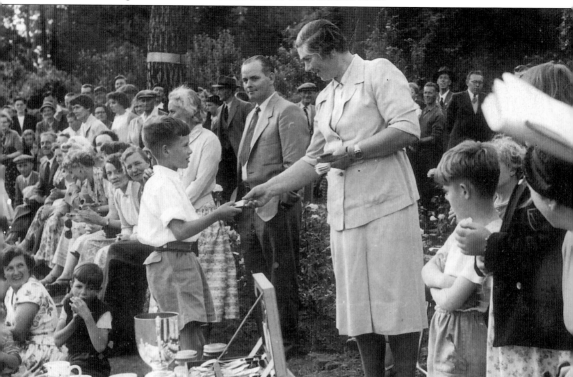

This is Lady Mary Grosvenor, who was the daughter of the 2nd Duke of Westminster, presenting prizes at Churton Sports Gala.

This is the Nurses Cottage in the village of Aldford. Although there was a nurse in the village in 1910, Miss Isabelle Kinney, this was not her address. In 1914 Miss Laura Payne, CMB midwife resided at Nurses Cottage.

Farndon Road and the Grosvenor Arms in 1907. Traditionally the village housed the artisans and skilled workers essential to the life of the Grosvenor Estate. Among the nameplates on the village fingerpost are Saightan, Chester, and Eaton Hall.

Streeton Mill is of a building type of which no other example remains in the county. An inscription on the west gable reads: 'This mill was built by Wm Leche Esq.; Jon. Harding, miller; Ed Beaven, millwright; Jas. Wilbm, mason, 1770.' The mill has two wheels, with two sets of machinery, and two pairs of stones to each. The east wheel is mounted internally, and is breastshot, the west wheel is external and overshot.

Although an old coaching inn with stables for up to sixteen horses, the Cock O' Barton, along with the Pheasant at Burwardsley, was better known for cockfighting. The walls in both inns have paintings and other items on their walls relating to this ancient sport.

Church Lane, Farnon in 1900. On 31 January 1900, five local men went to fight in the South African war, with another one following in April. In 1901 the men returned home safely, and a service of thanksgiving held in the parish church was attended by 450 people.

Outside the Greyhound in May 1914 is a horse apparently not required for war service! At one time the name was the 'Black Dog Inn '.

The Boat House stands almost on the river bank and occasionally has to be evacuated when the River Dee is in flood. At one time rowing boats were hired out here. The adjoining tearooms are still well patronised in the summer months.

The Farndon Bridge was built in the fourteenth century; it has nine arches, and the recesses on the bridge allow pedestrians to escape from passing vehicles. Until 1866 there was a toll and charges were: a dog on a lead ½d, a horse 1d, and a cart and horse 2d.

Five
Around Handbridge and Saltney

Old Dee Bridge. Where an upright pole sits in the top of the weir bank is the right-hand boundary of the weir gate. The weir is at the same height as that of a 28ft tide (at Liverpool), but at spring and winter high tides may exceed this by another couple of feet. At this time a gate may be opened in the weir giving a further 2ft in depth. A water engineer's presence is necessary to facilitate this service for boats wishing to pass through downstream.

The City and County School, Queen's Park, the headmaster was Mr J.K. Wilkins. The Under 14 X1 1932, from left to right, back row: T. Briggs, J.N. Craine, H.R. West, W.N. Higgins, J. Caldwell, D. Williams. Middle row: C. Tremlett, W.J. Williams, E.D. Greenway (captain), Mr Ramshaw, J.R. Wright, R.C. Rigby. Front row: C. Poole, B.F. Hobson.

The City and County School for Girls, Queen's Park, the headmistress was Miss H.M. Footman. Hockey XI 1932/33, from left to right, back row: D. Chalkley, B. Smith, E. Reynolds, J. Midge, D. Jarvis. Front row: M. Griffiths, M. Wilding, E. Large, G. Davies, M. Hewson, Miss Matthews. (absent: N. Ridgers)

Old Dee Bridge and Mills. The salmon boats go out in slack water when the incoming tide has stopped the rivers flow, the fisherman in the boat lays his net and his assistant holds the other end whilst standing on the bank. Eighteen licenses were issued annually, and each holder made his draw in strict rotation.

Handbridge. The season for net fishing opens at midnight on the last day of February, thought this depends which day this date falls on, for on the River Dee the law forbids net fishing on Fridays, Saturdays or Sundays. The fishermens' houses facing the river have long since gone.

Chester, St. Mary's Ch: Handbridge.

The house shown here is called 'Nowhere'. It was built over two hundred years ago by a man called Bingley and the name derives from its lonely position. Members of the Bingley family lived in it up until twenty years ago, when William Roberts took it over. Some years after this some more houses were built nearby. The nearest adopted the address No. 2 Nowhere, but after a court case they were refused permission to use the name.

Chester. King Edgar's Cave

Edgar's Field in Handbridge was presented to the city by the first Duke of Westminster in 1892. It was this sandstone outcrop which today is more discernible because it is now denuded of its vegetation overcoat; because of this the cave with its worn carving of the Roman Godess Minerva is more accessible. This was the Roman quarry used by them to build their Fortress of Deva (Chester).

A view not often seen on a postcard: an interior view of Eaton Hall Park. In the background on the right can be seen the famous Golden Gates. This view was taken in the 1920s. The writer on the back says, 'There are a lot of deer in the park'.

Members of the Earl of Chester's Imperial Yeomanry seem to have abandoned their traditional means of transport, the horse, for the first mechanised type. This photograph was taken on the 15 September 1911 when they were at camp in Eaton Park.

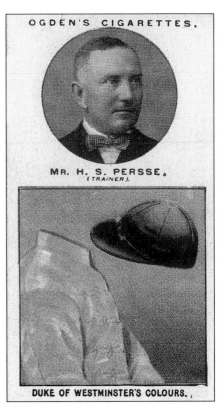

Two cigarette cards, *left*: The portrait of the 2nd Duke of Westminster as a young man was part of a set of 101 cards by Ogden's Guinea Gold Cigarettes. *Right*: This card is from the first series of 25 cards, 'Trainers and Owners Colours', showing the Duke's racing colours of gold jacket and azure cap based on the families original coat of arms, *The Bend Or* (The Golden Bend). Mr H.S. Perse was one of the Duke's trainers and had a large stable at Stockbridge.

HMS Tara was a converted Holyhead ship *SS Hibernia* which operated as an armed boarding cruiser in the First World War in the Mediterranean, when it was sunk by a German submarine. The eighty-six survivors were held prisoners by the Senussi tribe in the Libyan desert, and were rescued by a column of armoured cars led by the 2nd Duke of Westminster.

Eaton Laundry Fire. Posted in 30 December 1913 this postcard was sent from the laundry at Eaton Hall. The message reads: 'The fire was about four years ago, it started one Sunday in the engine house, whilst the girls were at church.'

This is a group of employees, both indoor and outdoor, of the Grosvenor Estate in a rare moment of leisure, in the 1930s.

Eaton Hall. The first one was built in 1700, followed by replacements in 1803-1812, was restructured 1845-1854, and then rebuilt in 1870-1883 by Alfred Waterhouse, at a cost of £600,000. Except for the clock tower it has now all gone. The new Eaton Hall is a more modern and modest building.

The Cadet School. At the end of the Second World War the army acquired the lease of Eaton Hall and grounds for fifty years at a peppercorn rent. However in 1960 due to a cutback in the armed services, the War Office asked to surrender the lease, which was granted. This is 'A' Company No. 5 Platoon at Eaton Hall in June 1956. The cadets all wear white collar flashes and in their berets is the badge of their parent regiment.

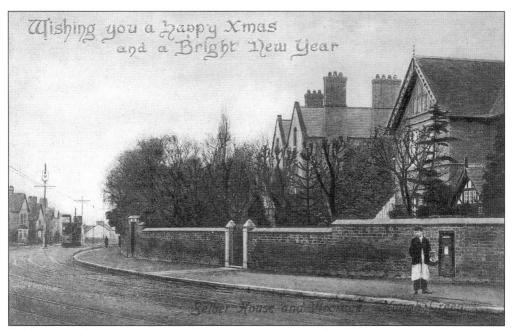

When postcards were overprinted, they were sometimes used as Christmas cards. This is a view of Seilber House and the vicarage, Hough Green. It was sent on the 21 December 1905, from the vicarage to the receipent in Ewart Street, Saltney Ferry.

This is horse tram car No. 4 about to leave Saltney Terminus in the late 1890s. Two horses were required to pull a full load up Chester Street hill. Then one horse would carry on into Chester, whilst the other would return to the Terminus, and await its next job. The young conductor is completing his waybill before departure.

Holly and Fern Villas. Saltney.

High Street, Saltney 1906, with St Anthonys School on the right. The school chapel was built in 1878 and continued in use until 1969 when a new school was opened.

This is the ship *Mary Cory* of Liverpool which broke loose from its moorings on the Spring Tide in September 1904 outside the tidal lock entrance into Chester Canal Basin.

SANDYCROFT WORKS. SHOWING THE SPOT WHERE THE „ROYAL CHARTER" WAS BUILT.

Royal Charter was originally planned as a sailing ship but her owners decided to lengthen her and add an auxiliary steam engine so that the ship could be used for transporting immigrants to Australia. Being launched sideways she got stuck and was damaged. After repairs she was relaunched in October 1855. Three years later she sank in a storm off Anglesey and today the ship's bell is on top of the Bluecoat School.

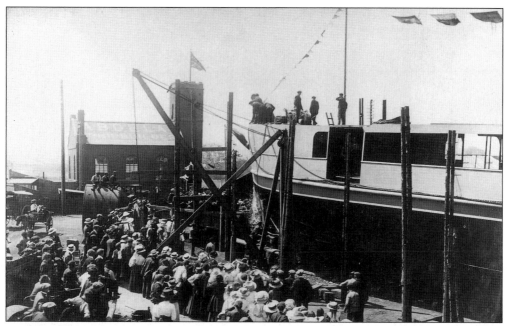

In 1852 George Cramm rented the River Dee Company Yard at Chester, and purchased Rigby's Sandycroft shipyard. Here he started the new side launching techniques that had been developed at Birkenhead. In the 1890s the yard was called Abdela Shipyards.

J. Crichton and Co. opened its shipyard in Saltney in 1913. Most of the vessels they built were shallow draught boats to use on rivers in tropical countries. This boat was the *R.H. Carr* built in 1927 for use in the Bahamas. The Crichton yard closed down in 1935.

When the *Quitador* was on its trials in the Mersey, she struck the steam barge *Doris* that was coaling up the Isle of Man steamer *Mona*. Before the *Doris* sank, her crew of four scrambled on board the *Quitador*, and eleven coal-heavers jumped on board the *Mona*.

The Mold Junction and Saltney Ferry Joint Strike Committee of Railwaymens' meeting on 4 September 1919. From left to right, standing: F. Moore, A. Liversage, J. Pleavin, J. Williams, E.J.T. Abram, J. Lawrence, J. Clark, A.G. Moyle, T. Keane, E. Farrel, F.R. Cofgreave, T. Thomas, S. Crocombe. Sitting: T. Liversage, O.J. Williams, F.J. Jones, J. Read, P.O. Price, H. Roberts (secretary), W. Pugh (chairman), J. Davies (vice-chairman), T. Parr, W.F. Burdett, W. Jones, J. Boulton.

The Saltney Ferry station and Mold Junction engine shed. The station opened in February 1891, and was the first station on the Chester-Mold branch. The shed was built in 1890, purely for servicing and maintaining the freight locos of the area. Around forty locomotives used to be shedded at any one time. The shed closed in April 1966.

A ganger and his gang of platelayers alongside their huts at Saltney Great Western shunt yards. This postcard was sent from Chester to Ellesmere, Salop, on 26 March 1911; the same background can be seen below, fifty years later.

A view of the Great Western pannier shunts yard in the early 1960s taken from Dee Junction signal box by the late Mr J. Butler.

This was the Coronation Scot running through Mold Junction (Saltney Ferry) in July 1937, on a LMS promotional tour. (Photograph by E. Beckett)

From 1920 until 1939 when the down Irish Mail arrived at Holyhead, the train guard would proceed to the mail boat before it departed for Ireland and show them on his watch the exact Greenwich Mean Time that it had been set to in London. If necessary the ships clocks would be adjusted accordingly.

William Henry Lindop was born 18 June 1843 in Crewe. For many years he was a driver of the Irish Mail when it was a single wheeler express on the Crewe-Holyhead section. When he was retired from that link his new job was driving *Tiny* the Crewe Work's narrow gauge locomotive.

Acknowledgements

First and foremost I would like to thank The Right Worshipful the Lord Mayor of Chester and Admiral of the Dee, Reggie Jones, for his kindness in writing a foreword for this book.

I would also like to thank the following for all their help with photographs and information: Mrs M. Beith; the late Mr J. Butler; R.M. Cash, secretary of Chester Boughton Hall Cricket Club; S. Courtney, Royal Naval Museum; John Dixon, railway historian; Geoff Ellis; Deryck Fairhurst; the late Ron Fleet, president of Chester Boughton Hall Cricket Club; Ted Gerry; Christine Gregory (Ms), Reprograpic Services Officer, Royal Air Force Museum; Mrs Jacqueline Halewood, Chester City archivist; Ken Hasall; Mike Hewitt; Ron Hignett; Miss A. Hodgson; Mark Johns; Reg Lindop; Arthur Moorcroft; the late Ray Mulligan, local history tutor; John Noble; Glynn Parry, author and local historian; Joyce and Bill Rowland; John Ryan; Derek Stanley, author, Lionel Smith; Geoff Taylor, canal historian; David St John Thomas, publisher; Fred Totty; John Whitingham, railway historian and the managers and staff of the Blossoms Hotel.

If I have omitted anyone who has helped, please accept my apologies.